MW00850282

SWIFT HOUR

WINNER OF THE 2012 ADRIENNE BOND AWARD FOR POETRY

MERCER
UNIVERSITY PRESS

Endowed by
TOM WATSON BROWN
and
THE WATSON-BROWN FOUNDATION, INC.

Advance Praise for *Swift Hour*

A great and sacramental silence hovers delicately above all the poems in Megan Sexton's first full-length collection. From the archetypal, tripartite structure the book employs—shell/nest/seed—to the poet's beautifully nuanced representations of the inarticulable generative forces at the center of all our human endeavors, the poems of *Swift Hour* bring us face to face with the painful beauties and joyous sorrows of those of us fortunate enough to live—as Megan Sexton clearly does—spiritually infused everyday lives.

> —Kate Daniels, author of four books of poetry
> and the recipient of the
> Hanes Award for Poetry
> from the Fellowship of Southern Writers.

Swift Hour, with its multiple connotations, is the perfect title, almost a preface, to this book. The poems swing-dance and they waltz, they're filled with rich ulteriority as well as a clarity of wonder, a kind of controlled abandon that only poets with real skills can achieve. This is a splendid debut collection. Godspeed *Swift Hour*, with rockets, into the world!

> —Thomas Lux, author of numerous books of poetry,
> most recently, *God Particles*, and
> recipient of the Kingsley Tufts Award

Megan Sexton's *Swift Hour* is infused with wonder at our world. Orpheus and Eurydice are spotted at a bus station. Akhmatova huddles with a friend who is memorizing the poem she doesn't dare keep on paper. Like Saint Thérèse of Lisieux, Sexton is dressed as Joan of Arc ready to do battle, whether that fight is of the mothers of the disappeared or a waitress who is transfigured as she serves her customers. Reading these poems we feel the terror of a bird trapped in a room and the exhilaration when the window is opened. Prepare yourself to be transformed by her quiet meditations on our perplexing moment in time.

> —Barbara Hamby, author of four poetry collections,
> including *All-Night Lingo Tango*,
> and recipient of the Kate Tufts Award.

The poems in Megan Sexton's *Swift Hour* have a fierce delicacy, whether they are describing the houses of Amsterdam, mothers mourning their disappeared children, or lovers "fused under the bedclothes." Her far-ranging imagination is both visual and conceptual, and the simple diction of her language belies the complexity of thought and feeling underneath. This is a wonderful book.

—Linda Pastan, the author of more than
twelve books of poetry and essays,
the recipient of Ruth Lily Poetry Prize,
and a two-time finalist for
the National Book Award.

"The poems in *Swift Hour* are lucid, serious, and deeply humane. To her credit, Megan Sexton writes without affectation or pretense. Stylistically speaking, the poems proceed in a deceptively simple, plainspoken way, but they go deep, examining the unseen spiritual underpinnings of the world we live in. Sexton's generosity of spirit shines forth on every page.

—Elizabeth Spires, the award-winning
author of six books for children
and six collections of poetry,
most recently, *The Wave-Maker* (2008).

SWIFT HOUR

Poems

MEGAN SEXTON

MERCER UNIVERSITY PRESS

MACON, GEORGIA

MUP/ P478

Published by Mercer University Press, Macon, Georgia 31207
© 2014 by Mercer University Press
1400 Coleman Avenue
Macon, Georgia 31207
All rights reserved

First Edition
Books published by Mercer University Press are printed on acid-free paper that
meets the requirements of the American National Standard for Information
Sciences—Permanence of Paper for Printed Library Materials.

Library of Congress Cataloging-in-Publication DataSexton, Megan.
  [Poems. Selections]
  Swift Hour : poems / Megan Sexton. -- First edition.
    pages cm
  ISBN-13: 978-0-88146-469-6 (pbk. : acid-free paper)
  ISBN-10: 0-88146-469-4 (pbk. : acid-free paper)
  I. Title.
  PS3619.E984A6 2014
  811'.6--dc23
                                        2014000359

Contents

Acknowledgments

Grateful acknowledgment is given to the editors of the publications in which some of these poems appeared: *The Alaska Quarterly, Birmingham Poetry Review, Calyx, The Iowa Review, Ploughshares, Poetry, Prairie Schooner, Rattle, The Irish Times, The Southern Review,* and *Willow Springs.*

"The Meaning of Bones" appeared in *Claiming the Spirit Within*

"Ramps" appeared in *Under the Rock Umbrella*

"Marriage Patois" appeared online in *Poetry Daily* and *The Poetry Daily Anthology.*

Thanks to Kevin Cantwell for including several of these poems in the chapbook *Insects & Mystics,* winner of the Redbone Press Award.

I would like to thank the Hambidge Center for Creative Arts and Sciences for the time I spent there. To my friends generous in their help and support of this book: David Bottoms, Andrea Carter Brown, Beth Gylys, Gregory Fraser, Barbara Hamby, Margaret Mills Harper, Scott Hightower, Alice Hoffman, Anya Silver, William Walsh, and most especially, Michael and Nora, heart and soul.

"I hope you're keeping some kind of record."
— Leonard Cohen

for Michael and Nora

SWIFT HOUR

1.

SHELL

The Narrow Houses of Amsterdam

To get to them, think in circles,
think of the skinny streets of dreams,
of paintings before the discovery of perspective,
before the first Baedeker was written,
roving at dusk, then midnight
along rows of cafés shelved like antique books;
think past the narrow houses of Amsterdam,
first spring, then summer, in a toy city,
a pop-up city with glass windows,
the linden trees, their leaves tarnished filigree,
the bicycles choking the streets,
and bells ringing out from handlebars,
bells ringing out from church towers,
past the houseboats bobbing on their anchors,
and the tulips spare in their beauty,
under street lamps where Spinoza polished his spectacles,
where none of my family ever visited,
where I came ten years ago and am now with you
standing in front of the narrow houses of Amsterdam.
Gezellig. My guide calls this warmth, well-being—
seeing behind the wimple of opened drapes
we are supposed to, allowed to, expected to,
look through each window, each wind's eye.

A Photo of St. Thérèse of Lisieux Dressed as Joan of Arc, 1894

> "I feel the call of an apostle. I'd live to travel all over the
> world, making Your name known."
> —Thérèse Martin

Before her sisters had gathered around
the white linens of her bed,
and clipped her fingernails,
thin as garlic skins,
collecting relics that they slipped
under their heavy mantles,
and some months before
the small sacs of her lungs
began to bleed and tear
like the withering wings
of a dying swallowtail,
she posed for her sister Leonie
as the maiden of Orleans.
Wearing home-made armor
over a skirt with her hair uncovered,
she acted out scenes from the crusader's life.

And in her eyes, a fire, a knowing
that her *alpargates* would tread only the cloister
and garden at Carmel.
Still there was something left
of the craving to whisper His name
while tied to the stake,
but instead she placed a portable desk
over her knees and began to write down words
—dense as attar of rose, light as her soul.
She made each day a small offering

of orisons, a bare floor cleanly swept,
and the notice of light and shade
intermingling along the convent walls.

The Folklore of Waitresses

That day swallows flew from God's mouth
down to earth.
They landed in the bare red oaks
outside the café.
Rumor was the sounds they made stopped cars.
Inside the small room
a waitress passed from table to table.
The smell of rosemary and sage fell out
of the pleats in her dress and embalmed the air
for miles around.

Behind her back, she heard the music
of people saying she looked so familiar.
On each of their plates she dropped
a handful of fresh herbs.
When the people ate,
they felt fuller than they had ever felt.
Their lives felt full then,
as if they would rise out of their bodies
and see themselves sitting there
with nothing to do. When she left them,
the birds broke into little flowers on the trees.

The Meaning of Bones

Twins of grief—
the mothers of the disappeared
march two by two
on the Plaza de Mayo.
They wear placard-size photos
of Luis, Claudio, and Lila
as necklaces
to remind the world
of their invisible children.

With their trowels
students dig down
in dumps and back lots
for cracked skulls,
the isolated pelvis,
a molar.

While the mothers pray
for the finality of forensics,
one mother begs the scientists
to display her daughter's skeleton
pieced together on a table.

Standing before them she weeps,
touching every bone,
dusting earth from the white china.

Lastochki

Beside a window for the light
they sat facing one another.
Akhmatova closed her eyes and recited
 the words that came to her
like sparrows landing on snow,
light and sudden, then gone.
A man wrote them quickly on cigarette paper
crackling in his hand,
the sound of a fire starting.

Always careful not to go for too long,
they both stopped. He read the words
over and over to her until they lived
inside themselves familiar as the dead's names.
He lit a match then burned the paper.
It glowed violet blue as the air consumed it.
They breathed deeply, living on what they couldn't see.

Orpheus and Eurydice at the Greyhound Station

I saw him pulling her off of the Greyhound bus, both of them looking like
they'd really been to hell and back. He wore a brown leather jacket that
hung on him like a bear skin. Her bones were lost in a matted fur coat, the
hem dragging behind her over the cracked asphalt. They carried no bags. As
I lurched toward the bus in my Jetta, both of them made eye contact with
me as they crossed over the yellow line, heading for the McDonald's across
the street. Something pulled my car to the left, so I coasted into the parking
lot, cut the engine, then sat there staring at them as they shuffled up to the
counter. He was propping her up like a mannequin—her balance had gone
out. I thought in an instant as the morning light poured down on the dull,
vanilla computer terminals that I had to know where they had returned
from and didn't want them to walk away from me until their bodies were
shapeless specks on the horizon.

Elegy for Chinese Couple

Forgive me, I looked at the gruesome photo
of you entwined on the sidewalk under a sheet,
your bare legs carelessly left uncovered, a bloom
of blood on the pavement next to you.

Instead, let us remember you both at the hotel
holding each other in mid-air behind the glass,
your embrace floating above
the chaos of the city below.

I try to imagine there was a mercy
in your shattered falling
like the night swifts mating in flight,
urged on by the velocity of love.

The Feast of Excited Insects

Tonight in our backyard it's so dark
I could have my eyes closed, a darkness
as if I'm wrapped and weighted in brown robes,
stunned by the ecstatic birds of Assisi.
For an instant, light floods into my heart
like the sun forcing its way through a window
into a room painted by Vermeer.
Cicadas spur the rattles of their tiny bodies,
each male beating a rhythm all his own,
each female rapt in a field of silence.
Ti voglio offrire tutto—
I would offer you everything.

Journey

The mind loosens its locks and slips,
dreams will repair, refresh, revise—
the brain is like a snail crawling
the rim of a hub cap.

How a baby's heel used as a pincushion
turns into a scene with you,
reappearing at the train station.
A ventriloquist's hand
moves me down the aisle
as we take our seat,
riding to a place faraway.
Snow blurs the windows,
then we arrive, the door opening on
zinc-white mountains, a sunny alpine town.

2.

NEST

Marriage Patois

After a thousand days,
our language is fixed
as the Madagascar-shaped mole
on your neck
and the pink levees
of your eyelids.
Like avid expatriates,
we're perfecting the accent
of our new country,
trading in the rug
of our old tongue.

I say fire the translators,
no more dictionaries.
We're natives now
because last night
I dreamt I stood
in our garden
and spoke my name for you.
With each sound,
one of my teeth fell out,
and from each glyph they made
in the dark loam,
a wild orchid grew.

Dream of the Orchard Thieves

Coiling around one another's body
like the ivy spiraling up the oak outside our window
we turn not knowing how many times—
back to breast, thigh to thigh on our bed
as if on the soft grass of Eden.
Both of us filled to the brim
with the fruit we'd gorged on earlier in the day,
our fingertips stained the color of figs,
faces slick with the residue of juice.
All forgiven now, under the wings of sleep.

Ramps

I find you in the soil-rich forest
behind brush, black brush.
You wash away my winter face—
my spring tonic,
I will smell like you
for five days.
School girls in Appalachia
get sent home for picking you
during recess.
I kneel under giant red oaks
before you, my wild leek,
my shy one.
When I take you,
the woods sway a little.

Robin

How perfectly you fit
into the landscape.
The brown of your back
and the burnt umber
of your breast matching
the dirt and leaves
you rummage through.
Always the first to sing,
and the last to stop.

I am like you,
a collector of paper,
a rummager,
sorting through
the underbrush,
stopping for no reason
other than to look
into the distance
as a jay flies
out of the pines.

Coney Island, c. 1929: Photograph by Walker Evans

All before was dark
like the inside of a camera.
Then the aperture opened—
my mother was born,
pulled through waves,
then a sudden sluice,
the blue air
of the delivery room
and a premonition of sky,
a nurse lifting her up,
as my grandmother
opened her eyes.

Just a few miles away,
Evans was closing silence
over the sound of the ocean
as a man and a woman
held one another,
their backs facing us,
a gap of water before them,
then the entrance to Luna Park.

The man, shirtsleeves
up to his elbows,
stretches his arm across her waist.
She's wearing a watch,
the band pinches her wrist.
Her skirt's got the wind in it.
The last bit of sunlight

is collecting around
the heels of their shoes.
We don't know if
they're coming or going.

Anniversaries

At dawn, the rustle of wings, as if God had cleared the surface
    of the Ganges with a sweep of his hand.

Half asleep, I hear the radio announcer describe a boat drifting by
    a small gathering of people at the river's edge.

In my dream schools of fish part to make room for its passage,
    its wake widens into nothing.

As the bow cuts through, cleaving a mark the river seems to repair,
    a river you knew enters my mind.

The Arno. Fishermen reeling in trout in the middle of the tide
    seems a dictum for how we wrestle thought.

Standing at the prow, Gandhi's great-grandson scatters ashes
    as chants rise up from the bank.

Men and women dive into the water, ash collects in the corners of their eyes,
    in the wells of their ears.

More people should be gathering at the shore, but instead they are sleeping.
    How will they know the light at dawn is like peace?

Visitation

Across the neighborhood the howls and cries
of dogs slip into the houses with children
coming home late for dinner.
The trees hold themselves further apart now
that their leaves have shed and scattered.
Seed pods and samaras scrape the sidewalks,
some force flinging them far from here.

Today a swallow trapped herself in my room,
flying over and over to the same window,
always stopping short of breaking it,
never quite making it through the door
I'd pulled open only inches away from her.
Until finally a fluttering under the bowl of sky.

To One Steeped in Folly

In this world,
you must move below the obvious.
A reality more like this—
after reaping all they could from the land,
men and women on the western frontier
would burn down their houses,
and after the fire died,
they'd pick through the ash for nails.

Ear Mouse

Some time passed.
Then an ear sprouted
on her back like a flower
and soon broke open
its canna blossom.
Now she trudges under its weight
on her back, carrying it around
into crevices between walls,
maneuvering under dressers
and couches.
She waits for the sounds
to collect in the canals
of flesh formed on her back.
She does not know why
she pauses as the funnel
of sound fills up
on her back
with a pressure
she can hardly bear.
Listening for lost apologies,
for all the garbled answers,
for all the half-whispered
protestations of love,
she must labor to move
what she's received
and lay it at the feet
of those who need to hear it,
of all those who are afraid
of what's dreadful and small.

In Favor of Union

"The steady evolution of the language seems to favor
union—two words eventually become one usually after a
period of hyphenation."

                                        —Strunk & White

I remember that brief period of hyphenation.
When separate cups held each of our toothbrushes,
and they bowed to one another honorably from across the vanity.
Now they nuzzle bristle to bristle, germ to germ, in the same cup
like so many words, each one suitable enough on its own—take *bed's*
monosyllabic brevity and slide it next to *chamber's* Old French spookiness
to make *bedchamber* and suddenly I'm thinking of swains and maidens and
European linens with extreme thread counts
and you and me, way beyond hyphenation, fused under the bedclothes.

Swift Hour

In this month of the saints and the dead,
I see explosions of swifts burst
from the magnolia trees downtown,
swooping by my ninth-story window.
My heart races with the black notes,
flying in patterns I have been blind to.
Dark arrows shooting in the direction of the fading sun,
pulling them towards it like shards of metal.

O Love, so much lies buried deep inside
until the trapped flue of the heart releases
thousands of flames silhouetted
across the evening sky.

3.

SEED

Ode to Silence

Glory to the half rest, to the breath between
  the third and fourth beats,
    the dwindling arrow of the decrescendo,

to the sunrise over Malibu, and its sleeping starlets,
  the empty horizon,
    the city's great thought still looming,

to parked cars, the cold engine seconds before ignition
  dreaming of the road
    unwound and endless,

to the lull before ecstasy, the saint's vigil
  of the dark soul in suffering,
    the grip of the heart before release,

to the inaction of love before the reaction,
  of the hand before it reaches out,
    its sharp twitch of self-consciousness,

to the embryo, the soft dream of the womb,
  the golden truth of genesis,
    the sustained hush and its amplitude.

My Daughter in the Fruits and Vegetables

She wants nothing to do with it,
recoils from its leathery skin,

a color she's never seen before—
red-pink and menstrual,

more squat than a pear, not quite an apple,
its obscene crown poking out of the crate.

Poison, she seethes, without me saying a word,
nothing of the myth lodged in my throat.

I keep my terror to myself
and will not sing the syllables

Persephone to her, for now, across the road,
wild violets still blanket the field.

First Bird

for Nora

Showing you the sparrows today for the first time
was like opening the small velvet box of my heart.
Those creatures of my childhood, who were always
patient to linger beside the curb or along the lid
of a garbage can just a few seconds longer
so I might glimpse their pied feathers.

Today I saw them light so easily along the edge
of the bus stop and pointed them out for you,
named them not birds, but sparrows,
and you grabbed for the song of the word.
Your eyes brightened as they flew for the boughs.
One day when you see them again,
you'll think their mottled wings could bear
your whole life up to the sky.

Parenthood

Our love has
made her
pearl of our flesh,
the grit of imperfection
polished now in her,
luminous, perfect
evidence.

Feeding the Shadow

Shadow, eat,
says the child
running to the dark figure
stretched before her,
tossing it a piece
of chicken meat,
dancing with it.
Spotting mine
next to hers,
she says she
will feed it too,
she will feed
all of the shadows
until they are not
hungry anymore.

Crabapples

I haven't thought of you for years, Patricia Kowalski, but I just read somet-
hing and remembered the crabapple tree in your backyard, nubby green
fruit littering the lawn, small and rotten, you made me take a bite—how I
hated you most of the time. Remember my father pummeling my bro-thers,
the five of them running in circles, like tramps in a silent movie? To where
have you dashed off? We pulled each other's hair until it clumped—fistfuls
of brown for you, yellow for me. Those strange plants growing beside your
carport—pink sacs dangling in sunshine. We held them up to our lobes like
earrings, and laughed when old Miss Wist called them bleeding hearts. Your
mother smacked you for squishing them on the drive. Bright red stains
lined the way from your house to mine. Where are you, oldest friend,
almost double? Thinking now of that place is like peer-ing out a plane
ascending to 30,000 feet—the higher we rise, the harder I squint to see.

Feathers

As if they'd fallen
out of the trousers
of the dead on the rise,
hundreds of feathers
cover this city's streets.

With the Radiance of Every Sun

for Dion

You lay in gold
as I sat by your bed.
I saw gold shedding
from your pores,
replacing sweat,
gilding the angles
of your bones.
Gold rose off of you
like heat from a cold river.
I no longer looked
at your body
as it sank
below the surface
of this world.
I saw only gold
and its message.
All things fell away—
as gold drew my eye
until you were all flame,
no wick.
You gave light
to the whole of the house
when gold lifted you
along the way.

Impressions

What if I could track
all the scars I've born
since childhood?
My skin a forest of cicatrix
like the constellations
we view over and over
in the night sky,
trying to make out an image.
Stars I've not seen for years
coming alive again.
They'd been there all along—
impressions,
like the pressed shadows
of Hiroshima
against statues of concrete.
We forget, until we remember.

Sea Sorrow

1.
What I weep now,
these tears,
how they are like the sea
we swam in when I was a girl
and you were the age I am now.
I think I was swimming
in tears, the blue vault
of the ocean,
nothing but tears.

2.
At the yoga studio,
we ended our sessions with sound,
each pregnant mother moving hands over
her belly like a crystal ball,
chanting with our eyes closed,
calling out to the child,
swimming within us.
Now I listen
for the hidden tones,
the faraway echo of your voice,
calling me in from long days
of play into the lighted house.

3.

I have three shells,
found long ago,
on beaches we'd visit.
Here's a gift,
the ocean said.
now I hold them
up to my ear,
listening to that place,
seeing us sea-soaked
and laughing.

Bottle of Tears

I thought they slipped into nothingness,
slid down the sides of my face,
vaporizing off the hard angles of my jaw.

But no, each one is collected,
harvested for safekeeping.
Imagine God's hundreds of windowsills,
lined with fluted glass, cut crystal,
bottles filled with tears, gleaming like baby teeth,
one labeled in script spelling your name.